BLUE WHALES

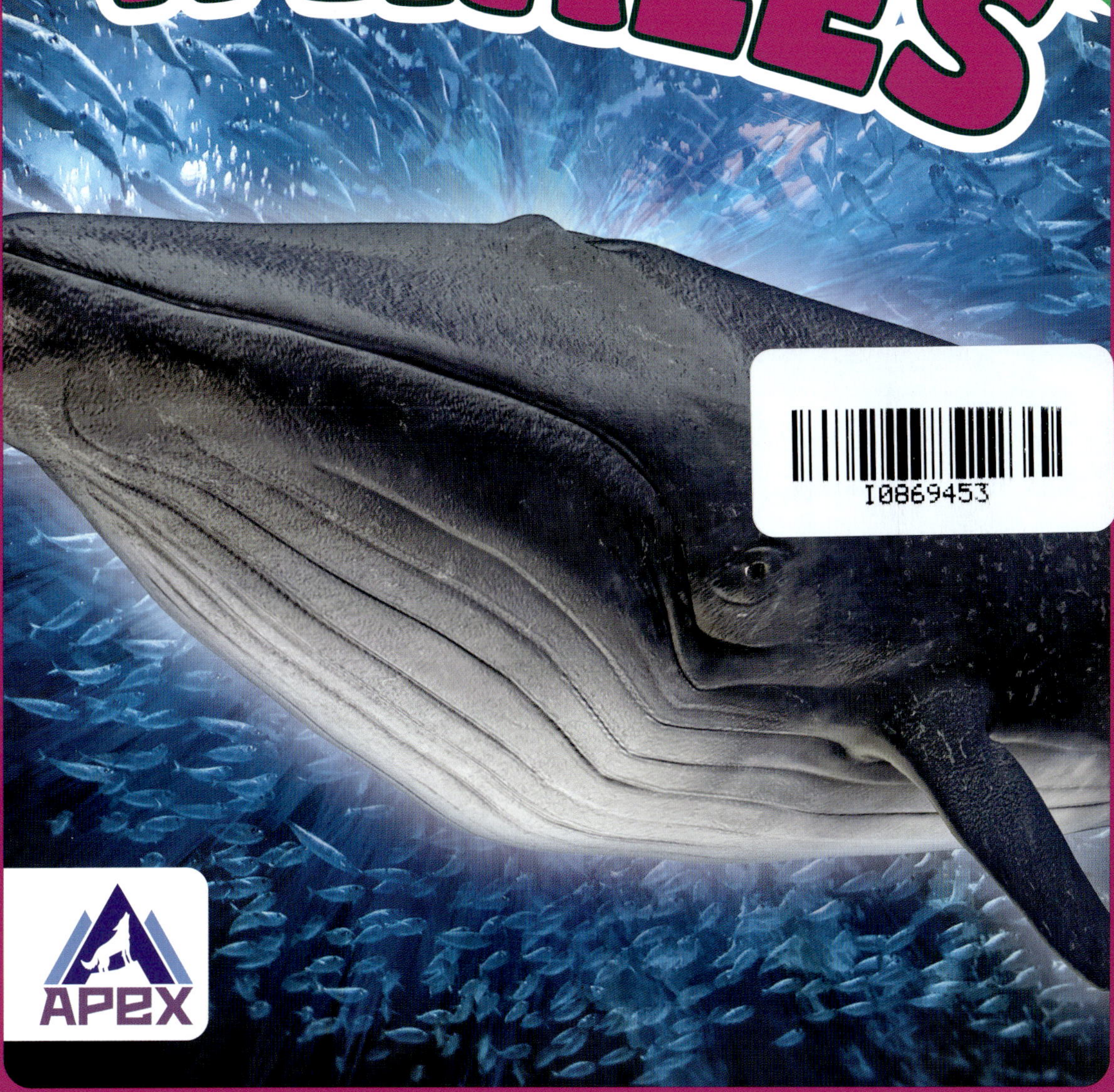

APEX

BY KATIE CHANEZ

WWW.APEXEDITIONS.COM

Apex is distributed by North Star Editions:
sales@northstareditions.com | 888-417-0195

Produced for Apex by Red Line Editorial.

Photographs ©: iStockphoto, cover, 1, 16–17, 20–21; Shutterstock Images, 4–5, 6–7, 8–9, 10–11, 12–13, 24, 25, 26–27; NOAA, 14–15, 29; The Natural History Museum, London/ Science Source, 18–19; Tony Wu/NaturePL/Science Source, 22–23

Library of Congress Control Number: 2020952977

ISBN
978-1-63738-002-4 (hardcover)
978-1-63738-038-3 (paperback)
978-1-63738-109-0 (ebook pdf)
978-1-63738-074-1 (hosted ebook)

Printed in the United States of America
Mankato, MN
082021

NOTE TO PARENTS AND EDUCATORS

Apex books are designed to build literacy skills in striving readers. Exciting, high-interest content attracts and holds readers' attention. The text is carefully leveled to allow students to achieve success quickly. Additional features, such as bolded glossary words for difficult terms, help build comprehension.

TABLE OF CONTENTS

CHAPTER 1

ON THE HUNT

A blue whale swims through the ocean. The huge animal is hungry. It spots **krill**. The whale opens its giant mouth.

Blue whales are the largest animals on Earth.

A blue whale can eat millions of tiny krill in one day.

Water rushes into the whale's mouth. Thousands of krill come with the water.

A blue whale's mouth could fit 100 people inside it.

The whale's tongue pushes the water back out. It flows through the whale's **baleen**. But the krill get trapped. The blue whale swallows them.

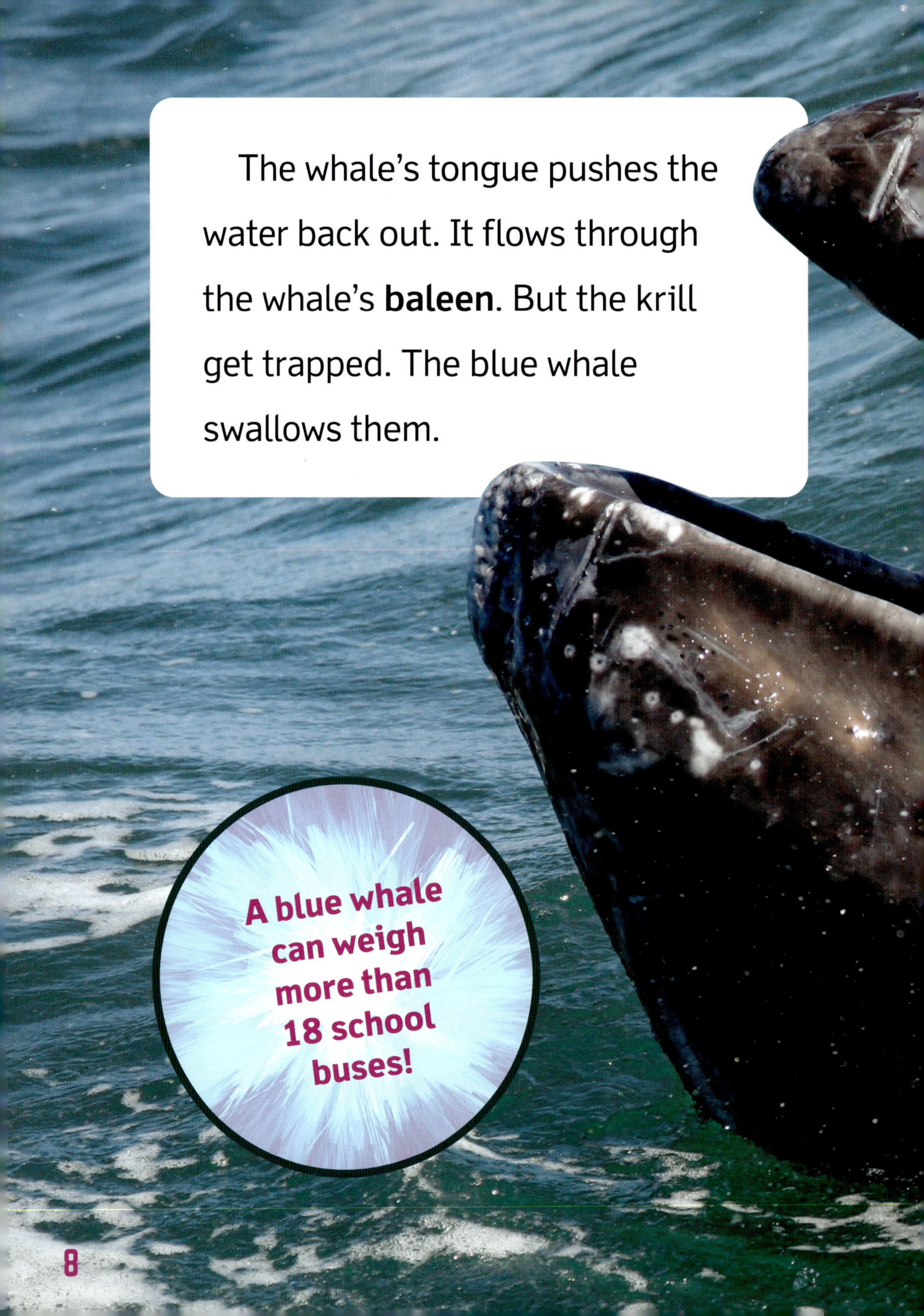

A blue whale can weigh more than 18 school buses!

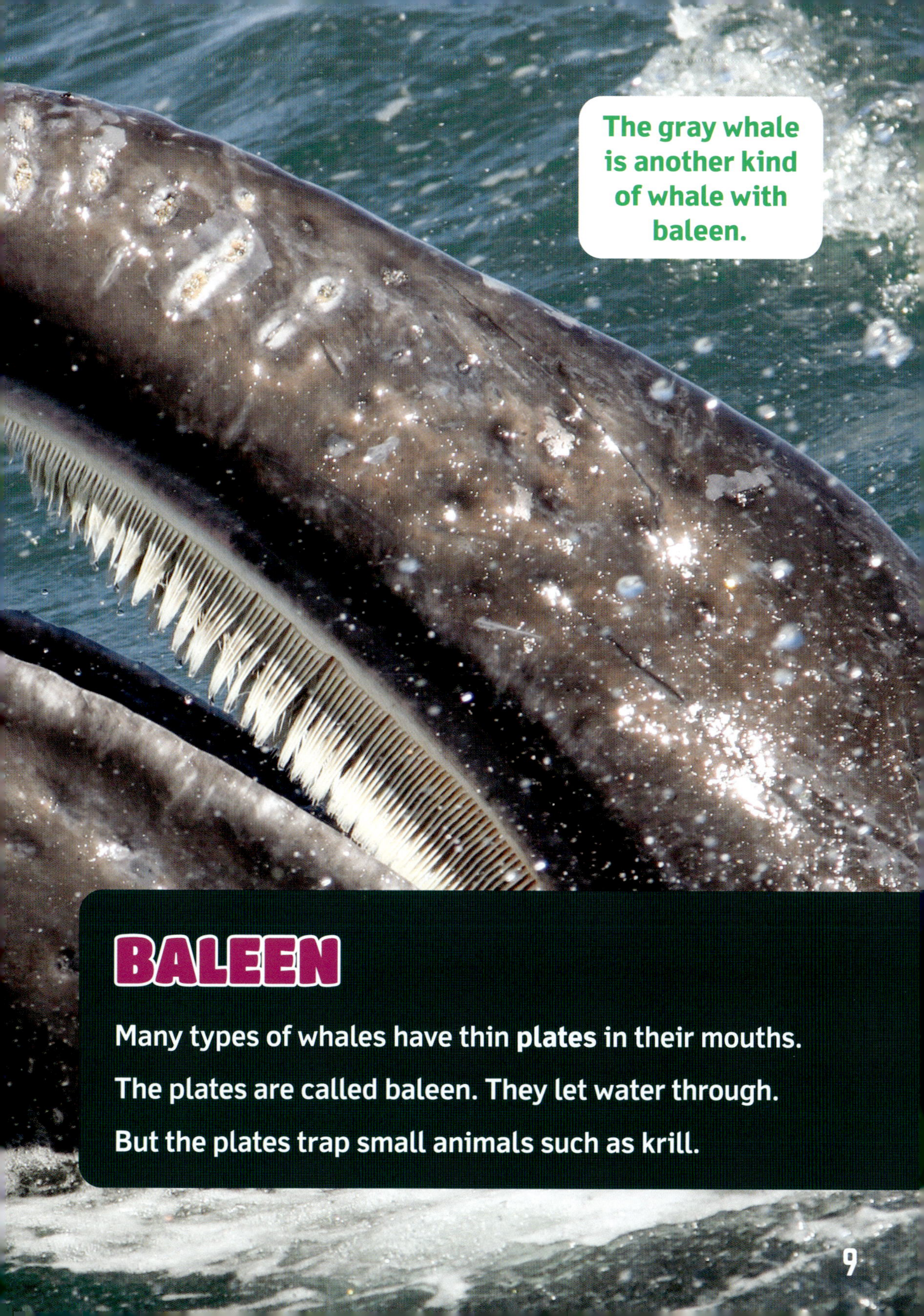

The gray whale is another kind of whale with baleen.

BALEEN

Many types of whales have thin **plates** in their mouths. The plates are called baleen. They let water through. But the plates trap small animals such as krill.

CHAPTER 2

OCEAN GIANTS

Blue whales can be more than 100 feet (30 m) long. That's longer than a basketball court.

Most blue whales are 70 to 90 feet (21–27 m) long. Some grow even bigger.

People often spot whales when they come to the surface for air.

Blue whales are **mammals**. This means they must breathe air. The whales swim to the surface to breathe. They can go an hour between each breath.

SWIM SPEEDS

Blue whales can swim up to 20 miles per hour (32 km/h). But they can't go that fast for long. They usually swim about 5 miles per hour (8 km/h).

A blue whale breathes through a blowhole. This opening is on the top of the whale's head.

Blue whales live in nearly every ocean. Some blue whales **migrate**. They move to warmer waters in the winter. Other blue whales live in the same place all year.

The largest blue whales live near Antarctica.

CHAPTER 3

WHALE SONGS

Most blue whales live alone. But sometimes they swim in pairs. Other times they swim in small groups.

Like blue whales, humpback whales swim in small groups called pods.

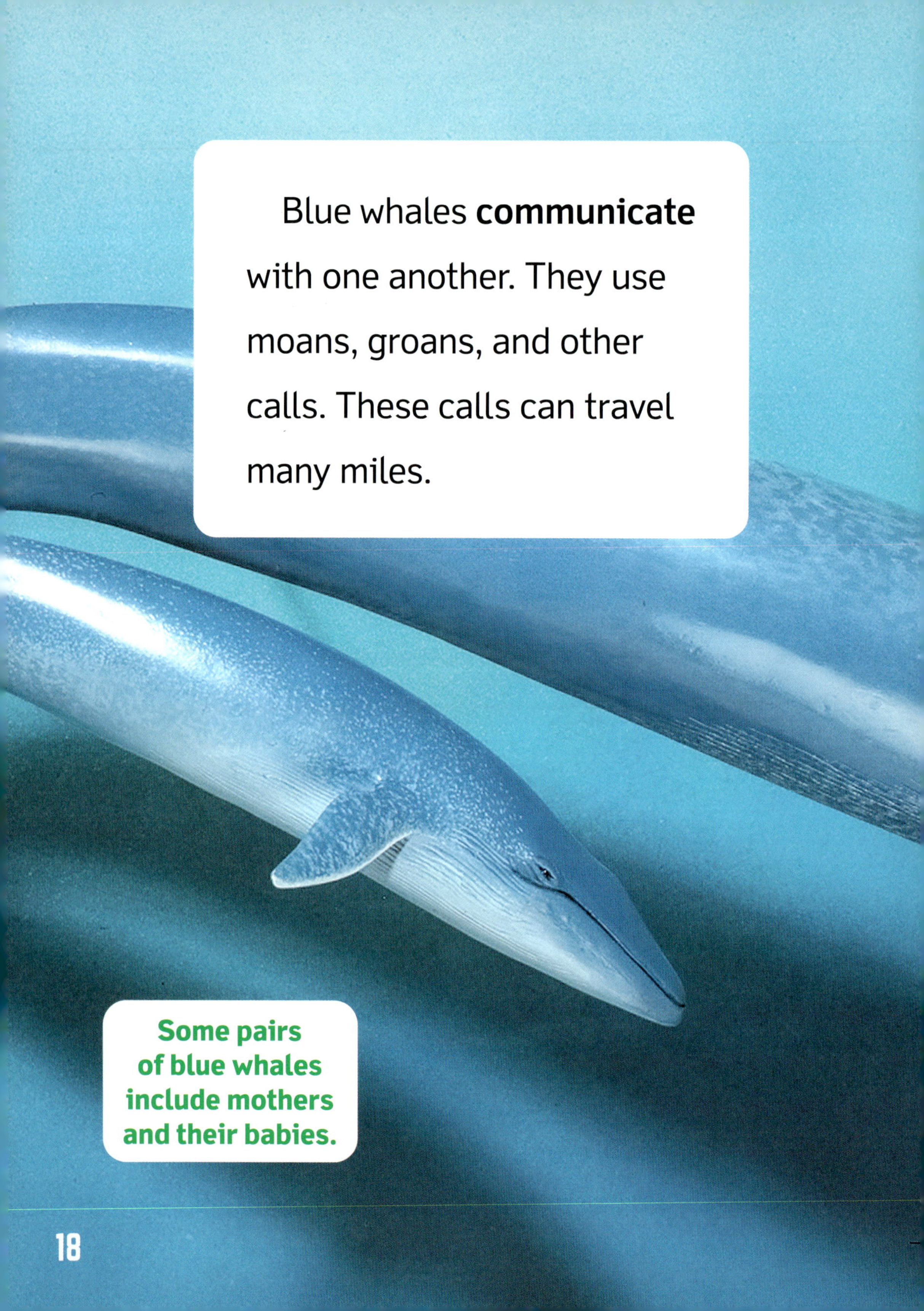

Blue whales **communicate** with one another. They use moans, groans, and other calls. These calls can travel many miles.

Some pairs of blue whales include mothers and their babies.

NOISY WATERS

More boats are in the ocean today than 100 years ago. Boat noise can cause problems for whales. It can stop whales from hearing one another. It can also change how they swim.

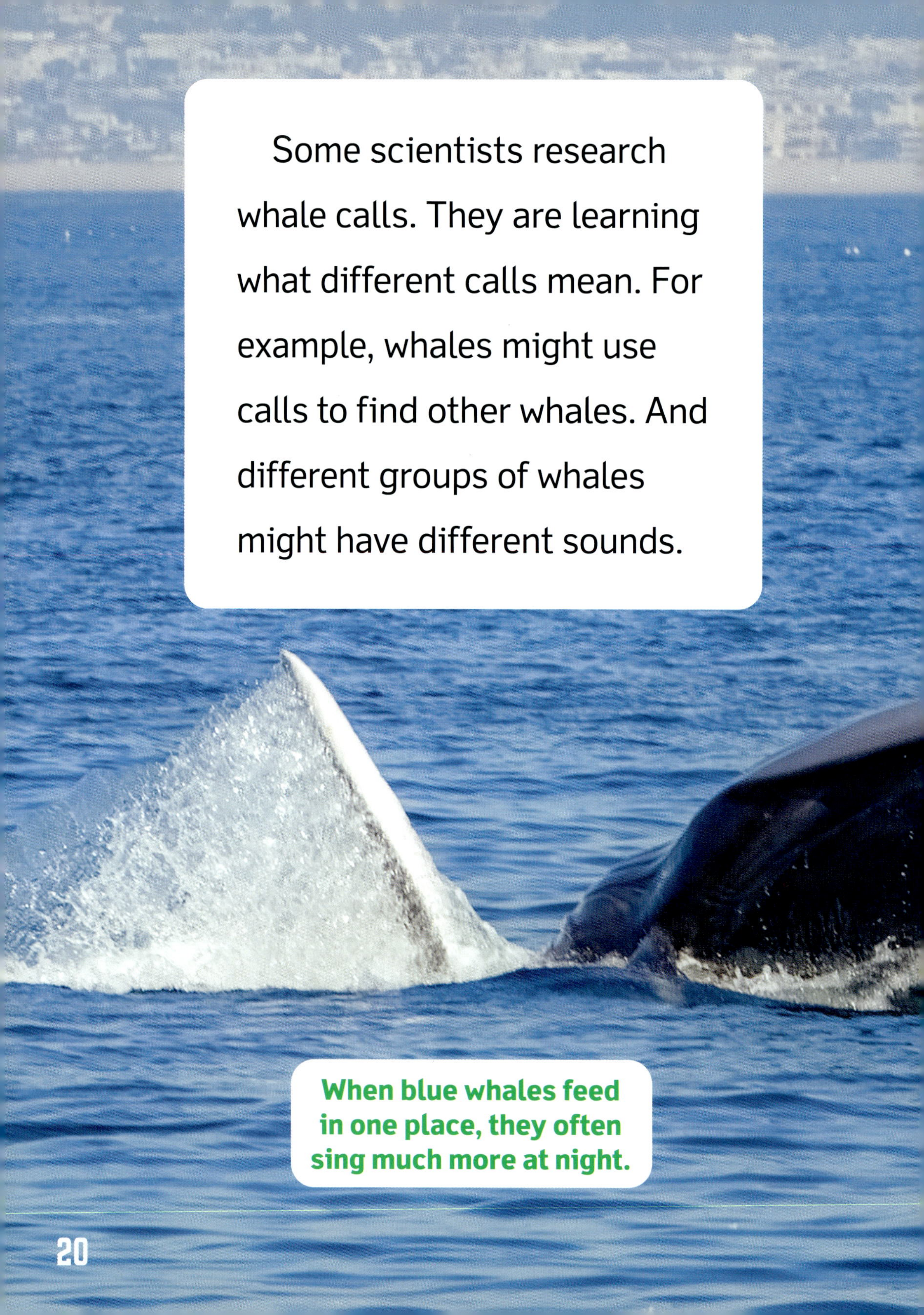

Some scientists research whale calls. They are learning what different calls mean. For example, whales might use calls to find other whales. And different groups of whales might have different sounds.

When blue whales feed in one place, they often sing much more at night.

A blue whale can be louder than an airplane.

CHAPTER 4

BLUE WHALES AND HUMANS

Blue whales are **endangered**. That's mainly because of humans. In the past, many people hunted the whales. As few as 10,000 blue whales are left.

Blue whales can live to be more than 80 years old.

Hunting whales is now **illegal**. But people can still hurt whales. Boats sometimes hit them. Blue whales can also get caught in fishing nets.

Many people travel on boats to see whales.

Many blue whales are hurt or killed when large ships crash into them.

KRILL FISHING

People fish for krill. Krill can be used to make animal food. But taking krill from the ocean leaves less food for whales to eat.

People are learning how to keep whales from getting stuck in fishing nets.

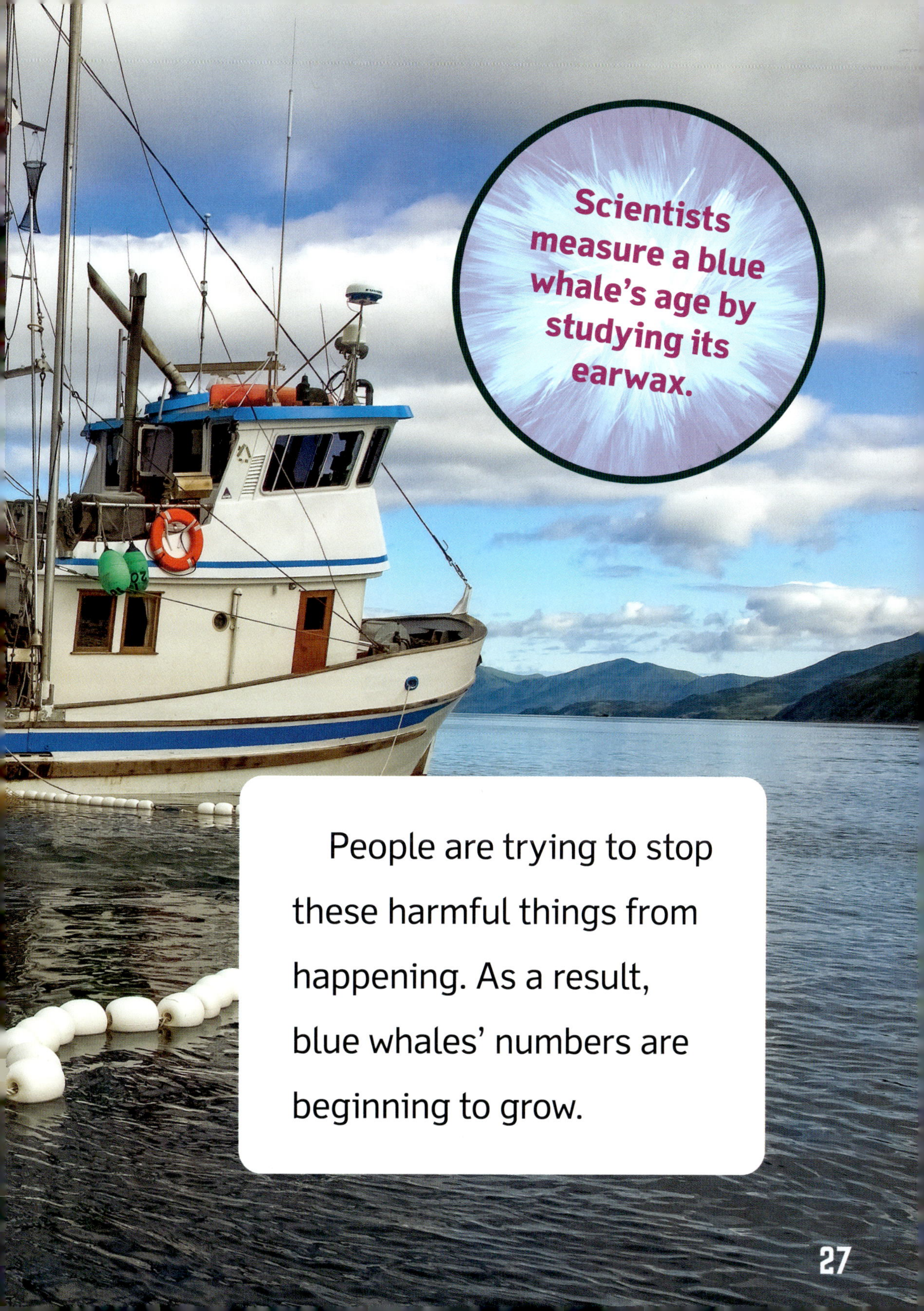

Scientists measure a blue whale's age by studying its earwax.

People are trying to stop these harmful things from happening. As a result, blue whales' numbers are beginning to grow.

COMPREHENSION QUESTIONS

Write your answers on a separate piece of paper.

1. Write a sentence that describes the key ideas from Chapter 4.
2. Would you ever want to swim with a blue whale? Why or why not?
3. How long can blue whales become?
   - **A.** less than 10 feet (3 m)
   - **B.** about 40 feet (12 m)
   - **C.** more than 100 feet (30 m)
4. How did blue whales become endangered?
   - **A.** Sharks attacked too many blue whales.
   - **B.** People fed blue whales too much food.
   - **C.** People hunted too many blue whales.

5. What does **research** mean in this book?

*Some scientists **research** whale calls. They are learning what different calls mean.*

A. to get lost
B. to study
C. to stay away from

6. What does **moans** mean in this book?

*They use **moans**, groans, and other calls. These calls can travel many miles.*

A. big, round eyes
B. loud, low sounds
C. short, thick fur

Answer key on page 32.

GLOSSARY

baleen
Plates that some whales have instead of teeth. They help whales catch food from the sea.

communicate
To send and receive messages.

endangered
In danger of dying out forever.

illegal
Against the law.

krill
Small animals that float in the sea. They look like shrimp.

mammals
Animals that have hair and produce milk for their young.

migrate
To move from one part of the world to another.

plates
Things that are smooth, flat, and thin.

TO LEARN MORE

BOOKS

Gish, Ashley. *Blue Whales*. Mankato, MN: Creative Education, 2019.

Murray, Julie. *Blue Whales*. Minneapolis: Abdo Publishing, 2020.

Schuh, Mari. *Blue Whales*. North Mankato, MN: Capstone Press, 2020.

ONLINE RESOURCES

Visit **www.apexeditions.com** to find links and resources related to this title.

ABOUT THE AUTHOR

Katie Chanez is a children's book writer and editor originally from Iowa. She enjoys writing fiction, playing with her cat, and petting friendly dogs. Katie now lives and works in Minnesota.

INDEX

Answer Key:
1. Answers will vary; **2.** Answers will vary; **3.** C; **4.** C; **5.** B; **6.** B